The Story of
His Glory

The Story of His Glory

Brian G. Hedges

:: CROSSWAY®

WHEATON, ILLINOIS

Published by Crossway
               1300 Crescent Street
               Wheaton, Illinois 60187

Much of the material in this book began as a gospel presentation by Brian G. Hedges for Revive Our Hearts website, https://www.reviveourhearts.com/gospel-story. It was also posted as "The Story of His Glory," September 12, 2013, www.brianghedges.com (blog), https://www.brianghedges.com/2013/09/the-story-of-his-glory.html.

Cover design: Jordan Singer

First printing 2019

Printed in the United States of America

Trade paperback ISBN: 978-1-4335-6436-9

Library of Congress Cataloging-in-Publication Data
Names: Hedges, Brian G., author.
Title: The story of his glory / Brian G. Hedges.
Description: Wheaton, Illinois : Crossway, 2019. | Includes index.
Identifiers: LCCN 2018027632 | ISBN 9781433564369 (tp)
Subjects: LCSH: Bible—Theology.
Classification: LCC BS543 .H4325 2019 | DDC 230/.041—dc23
LC record available at https://lccn.loc.gov/2018027632

Crossway is a publishing ministry of Good News Publishers.
VP   29 28 27 26 25 24 23 22 21 20 19
15 14 13 12 11 10 9 8 7 6 5 4 3 2 1

To my kids
Stephen, Matthew, Susannah,
and Abby Taylor

May your minds be shaped and
your hearts be transformed by
the wonder and beauty of the
glorious gospel of Jesus Christ.

Contents

The Story of
His Glory

+

We love stories. This is true of children and adults in every culture of the world.

Stories are important because they are the lenses through which we see the world. According to the philosopher Alisdair MacIntyre, "I can only answer the question 'What am I to do?' if I can answer the prior question

'Of what story or stories do I find myself a part?'"[1]

We make sense of both our personal and social identities through stories. If you want to really know someone, you ask them to tell their story.

Stories move us more deeply than mere explanations. Stories capture our imaginations, stir our hearts, and infuse our lives with meaning and significance.

In this little book, I want to tell you a story. It is the story of God's gracious rescue of the world through the gift of his Son and the sending of his Spirit. It is a story of creation and judgment, crime and punishment, grace and glory. It is a story filled with drama, tension, power, beauty, and hope.

This story is true and is found in the narratives, laws, parables, poems, sermons, songs, visions, prophecies, oracles, and letters that make up the sixty-six books of Scripture. At the heart of this story is the revelation of God's glory in the death and resurrection of his Son, Jesus.

This story, the story of God's glory, is the most important story in all of human history. And it is a story that can change your life.

This is that story in a nutshell.

The Creator God

The story begins with this simple sentence: "In the beginning, God created the heavens and the earth" (Gen. 1:1).

God is the Creator. This defines everything.

This means that your life is not an accident or a mere product of chance. The Creator God created everything. By his powerful and creative word, he spoke the universe and everything in it into existence (see Heb. 11:3).

> All things were made through him, and without him was not any thing made that was made. (John 1:3)

This truth has massive implications for us. If God is our Creator, then we are his creatures. We belong to him. A sculptor is the master of his clay. A painter is sovereign over her painting. An inventor retains the ownership rights over his invention. And in a similar way, God is the supreme owner of the universe and everything in it. He is the "possessor of heaven and earth" (Gen. 14:19). He creates and sustains our lives.

> In him we live and move and have our being. (Acts 17:28)

We can no more exist without God than a drawing can exist apart from the artist's hand.

Made for His Glory

If God is our Creator, then we were made for his purposes and pleasure (see Rev. 4:11). This is, in fact, what Scripture declares. We were made for God's glory and fame (see Isa. 43:7). Our purpose in life is to display the worth and value of the God who designed and created us. As an old catechism says, "Man's chief end is to glorify God, and to enjoy him forever."[2]

Made in God's image (see Gen. 1:26–27), the intended role of every human being is to be God's image-bearer—a portrayal of his character, a reflection of his glorious worth. This means human beings are like mirrors—made to reflect the beauty of another, the beauty of God.

God has also shown us what it looks like to reflect his glory in our lives. He has revealed this in his Word, beginning with his commands to the first human beings to "be fruitful and multiply and fill the earth," and to exercise dominion over it (Gen. 1:28). We were created to glorify God by extending his kingly reign throughout the earth, through living in loving obedience to his good commands and in harmonious relationships with one another (see Gen. 2:15–25). A fuller description of how to live was contained in God's divine law, which was revealed to his people Israel and expounded by teachers, sages, and prophets in the Old Testament.

Jesus summarized God's law in two great commands: "You shall love the Lord your God with all your heart and with all your soul and with all your mind. . . . [And] you shall love your neighbor as yourself" (Matt. 22:37–39). A life fully defined by love—supreme and total love for God and others—is a God-glorifying life.

Humanity Shattered by Sin

But humanity has fallen. Adam and Eve, the first human beings, disobeyed God (see Gen. 3:1–7). Sin intruded into God's good creation and therefore death invaded human history.

> Sin came into the world through one man, and death through sin, and so death spread to all men because all sinned. (Rom. 5:12)

Sin didn't stop with Adam. We all have sinned and fallen short of God's glory (see Rom. 3:23). We have traded the glory of the Creator God for created things and have loved and worshiped the creation more than the Creator (see Rom. 1:23–25). We have forsaken God, "the fountain of living waters" for "broken cisterns that can hold no water" (Jer. 2:13). The hearts of men are idol factories,[3] and we have all loved idols more than the living God. Idols can be self, sex, money, power, prestige, and pleasure, anything that holds greater significance in our lives than God.

Our problem is not merely sinful actions but sinful hearts. Jesus taught that it is "out of the abundance of the heart" that the mouth speaks (Matt. 12:34). As diseased trees will bear corrupt fruit, so diseased hearts bear the corrupt fruit of sinful attitudes, desires, motives, words, and behaviors.

Jesus said, "The good person out of his good treasure brings forth good, and the evil person out of his evil treasure brings forth evil" (Matt. 12:35). What is inside comes out.

> But what comes out of the mouth proceeds from the heart, and this defiles a person. For out of the heart come evil thoughts, murder, adultery, sexual immorality, theft, false witness, slander. These are what defile a person. (Matt. 15:18–20)

We have not loved God supremely. And we have not loved our neighbors as ourselves. By human standards, we may have lived respectable and moral lives, but deep in our hearts we know that even our best behavior has often been driven by self-serving motives and tainted with sinful desires. The Scriptures remind us that "whoever keeps the whole law but fails in one point has become guilty of all of it" (James 2:10). It only takes one drop of cyanide to poison a glass of water, and similarly even one sin leaves us guilty before a holy God. Jesus's teaching reached beyond behavior to the heart. He showed that hatred in the heart was murderous and that lustful thoughts were adulterous (see Matt. 5:21–29).

In our sinful hearts and actions, we have committed mutiny and treason against the Creator God. We have provoked God's holy wrath, sold ourselves into slavery to sin, and rendered ourselves incapable of fulfilling our divinely given purpose to glorify God (see Rom. 2:4–5; 6:16). We are "dead in . . . trespasses and sins" (Eph. 2:1), blinded by Satan, "the god of this world" (2 Cor. 4:4), and slaves of our passions and desires (see Eph. 2:2–3). If by creation man is a mirror made to reflect the radiance of God's beauty and glory, then sin has shattered that mirror.

The Covenant God

But the Creator God is also a covenant God—meaning he is a God of promise. Even before man's fall into sin, God had formed a plan of rescue (see Titus 1:2). He revealed that plan years ago to a man named Abraham.

Though he was old and childless, God promised Abraham a son and a family through whom all the peoples of the earth would be blessed (see Gen. 12:1–3; see also Genesis 15, 17). The promised son was Isaac, and the promised family became the nation of Israel. God chose Israel to be his special people, and he rescued them from enslavement in Egypt by his mighty hand (see Exodus 1–15). Later, the greatest earthly king of Israel was named David. To David, God also made a covenant, promising him a son who would be forever enthroned over his people (see 2 Samuel 7). The entire story of the Old Testament is the outworking of these two covenant promises; it is the story of God's glory returning to earth through his chosen people.

This story reaches its climax in Jesus, "the son of David, the son of Abraham" (Matt. 1:1). Jesus of Nazareth, born of a virgin in fulfillment of God's promises, was the true and promised offspring of Abraham, the true and promised Son of David (see Matt. 1:18–25; Rom. 1:3; Gal. 3:16). He was the *messianic* (meaning *anointed*) king who would rescue God's people from sin and death, inaugurate God's kingdom, and restore God's creation. Jesus was the ultimate revelation of God's glory, the true image bearer of God on earth. As the apostle John declared, "The Word became flesh and dwelt among us, and we have seen his glory, glory as of the only Son from the Father, full of grace and truth" (John 1:14). Jesus was God himself in human flesh.

The Crucified and Risen Messiah

For thirty years, Jesus lived a quiet Galilean life in the backwaters of Israel. Then Jesus burst on the public scene, proclaiming the gospel (or good news) of the kingdom, the fulfillment of God's covenant promises to his people (see Mark 1:15; Luke 4:17–21). Jesus's entire life was characterized by perfect love, obedience, and righteousness. He was, in fact, the "second man" and the "last Adam" (see 1 Cor. 15:45–49). Unlike the first Adam who was tempted and fell into disobedience, sin, and death, Jesus as the last Adam was tempted in every respect as we are, yet lived without sin (Heb. 4:15). He was our representative, whose sinless life and perfect obedience would bring life and salvation (see Rom. 5:12–21).

During his ministry, Jesus gathered followers and demonstrated both compassion and great power through many miracles, which served as inaugural signs of God's reign breaking into human history. He taught with authority, finding appeal among the common people and suspicion among the religious and political leaders of his day. He came with a message of hope, offering forgiveness and rest to those burdened and wearied with sin (see Matt. 9:1–12; 11:28–30). He claimed divinity and oneness with God (see John 10:30) and modeled a life of perfect love to God and man—always seeking the honor of his Father and extending mercy and compassion to broken people.

But his claim to be one with God eventually led to his death. Betrayed by the kiss of a friend and tried in a kangaroo court, Jesus of Nazareth was sentenced to death by crucifixion on a cross—the most degrading and agonizing form of capital punishment known in the ancient world. A Roman governor named Pontius Pilate declared Jesus's innocence yet still sanctioned his execution (see

John 19:1–16). Jesus died outside of Jerusalem sometime around AD 30 and was buried in the borrowed tomb of a man named Joseph of Arimathea. His disciples were disillusioned and discouraged, many of them having denied and forsaken him during the last hours of his life.

But three days later, his tomb was empty. Jesus came back to life and rose from the dead! For forty days, he appeared again and again to his disciples and closest friends, giving them comfort, commissioning them with a new mission, and promising them the empowering presence of the Holy Spirit. Then he ascended into heaven with the promise that one day he would return again.

The Good News

But what did it all mean? One of Jesus's followers, named Paul, was a deeply religious man who had persecuted Christians before encountering the resurrected Jesus himself. That encounter utterly changed Paul's life and he became an apostle (see Acts 9; 26:9–20; Gal. 1:10–24). In his letters to Christian churches, Paul reflected extensively on the meaning of Jesus's death, burial, and resurrection. These events were the core of the gospel— the good news—that Paul and the other early followers of Jesus spread to both Jews and Gentiles. Paul said, "For I delivered to you as of first importance what I also received: that Christ died for our sins in accordance with the Scriptures, that he was buried, that he was raised on the third day in accordance with the Scriptures" (1 Cor. 15:3–4).

Paul, and the other apostles, emphasized not just the *fact* of Jesus's death, but also the *reason*. He died *for our sins*. They realized that the death of Jesus resulted not just from the insidious plot of wicked men, but also from the eternal plan of God to rescue "people from their sins" and bring healing to the world (Matt. 1:21; see Acts 2:23; 4:26–28). Jesus himself had said that he came "to give his life as a ransom for many" (Mark 10:45).

The death and resurrection of Jesus was, in fact, God's solution to the problem of sin. Humanity was alienated from the Creator God. But God was in Christ, reconciling the world to himself by not counting our trespasses against us (see 2 Cor. 5:19). Instead he made Christ, who knew no sin, to become sin on our behalf, that "we might become the righteousness of God" in him (2 Cor. 5:21). God treated his sinless Son Jesus as if he had lived a sinful life, so that he could treat sinners as if they had lived the sinless life of Jesus. Through his crucifixion, Jesus satisfied God's wrath against sin so that God could be just in forgiving sin and declaring sinners righteous in his sight (see Rom. 3:25–26; 1 John 2:2). By "becoming a curse for us," Jesus delivered us from "the curse of the law" we had broken (Gal. 3:13). The one who was righteous (Jesus) died for the unrighteous (us), so that we could be restored to a right relationship with God (see 1 Pet. 3:18).

When Jesus rose from the dead, it was proof that he had conquered sin and death once and for all. Death could not hold him in its grasp (see Acts 2:24)! Death was defeated (see 1 Cor. 15:54–57). Jesus destroyed Satan who had the power of death, delivering "those who through fear of death" had been "subject to lifelong slavery" in sin (Heb. 2:14–15).

Responding to the Good News

When Peter shared the good news of Jesus's death and resurrection, people asked, "What shall we do?" (Acts 2:37). How should *you* respond to the news?

First, you must recognize your accountability to the Creator God. You were made by him and are owned by him. You are not the cause of your own existence. He is. And you were made for a purpose—his purpose. You were made to glorify him. But you—like all human beings—have failed to live for that purpose. None of us have lived for God's glory; we have all lived for ourselves. As the Bible says, "All we like sheep have gone astray" (Isa. 53:6). You have rebelled against the Creator and deserve his just judgment and condemnation. Because of sin, you are under the sentence of death, and after death you will face judgment (see Rom. 6:23; Heb. 9:27).

You must also realize that there is nothing you can do to rescue yourself from this judgment. Some people mistakenly think that they can earn God's favor by living good lives. Others suppose that they can escape judgment through observing some kind of religious ceremony. But Scripture teaches that neither good works nor religious observances are sufficient to save. Like an x-ray machine that can reveal a fractured bone but has no power to set it straight, God's holy law reveals our sinfulness to us—but is powerless to deliver us from our sin.

For by works of the law no human being will be justified in his sight, since through the law comes knowledge of sin. (Rom. 3:20)

Someone once said that there are two kinds of people who go to hell: the *un*righteous and the *self*-righteous. Living a moral life will not rescue you from sin. Neither will baptism, confirmation, giving to the poor, or going to church. Religion is simply a "more respectable" pathway to eternal destruction. The only candidates for salvation through Jesus are those who realize their utter helplessness to save themselves (see Luke 18:9–14).

Self-salvation is utterly impossible.

But what is impossible with man is possible with God (see Matt. 19:26). The crucified and risen Messiah, Jesus of Nazareth, the God-man, has done for sinners what they cannot do for themselves. When a jail keeper in the city of Philippi asked Paul and his companions, "What must I do to be saved?" they answered, "Believe in the Lord Jesus, and you will be saved" (Acts 16:30–31).

Believing in Jesus is more than merely acknowledging the fact of Jesus's existence or the truthfulness of his claims. Believing in Jesus is trusting in him, putting your faith in him. Someone once defined *faith* with the following acronym

Forsaking
All
I
Trust
Him

This is what it means to believe. In Paul's words,

> Whatever gain I had, I counted as loss for the sake of Christ. Indeed, I count everything as loss because of the surpassing worth of knowing Christ Jesus my Lord. For his sake I have suffered the loss of all things and count them as rubbish, in order that I may gain Christ and be found in him, not having a righteousness of my own that comes

from the law, but that which comes through faith in Christ, the righteousness from God that depends on faith. (Phil. 3:7–9)

Trusting in Jesus is not just the confession of a *creed*, but also the pledge of allegiance to a *person*. Jesus said, "If anyone would come after me, let him deny himself and take up his cross daily and follow me. For whoever would save his life will lose it, but whoever loses his life for my sake will save it" (Luke 9:23–24). Following Jesus involves receiving him as both Savior and Lord, trusting him to deliver us from both the penalty of sin and its power in our lives. The life of faith is a life of repentance. In Paul's words, the Christian message is one of "repentance toward God and of faith in our Lord Jesus Christ" (Acts 20:21). Trusting in Jesus involves turning—turning *from* sin and self-righteousness and turning *to* Jesus as Savior and Lord.

If you are to be rescued from God's just judgment on your sin and rebellion against your Creator, then you must ask the Lord Jesus to save you.

> Everyone who calls on the name of the Lord will be saved. (Rom. 10:13)

This is the promise of God.

> If you confess with your mouth that Jesus is Lord and believe in

> your heart that God raised him
> from the dead, you will be saved.
> (Rom. 10:9)

Repenting of your sins and trusting in Jesus is both God's invitation and his command.

> The times of ignorance God overlooked, but now he commands all people everywhere to repent, because he has fixed a day on which he will judge the world in righteousness by a man whom he has appointed; and of this he has given assurance to all by raising him from the dead. (Acts 17:30–31)

Will you obey his command?

Life in the New Creation

> If anyone is in Christ, he is a new creation. The old has passed away; behold, the new has come. (2 Cor. 5:17)

This is true for all who have been rescued by Jesus from sin. How can you know that you are a new creation? The Bible describes this newness in several ways. First, you will have a new relationship with the *Son of God*—Jesus himself. Following Jesus is not a one-time decision but a new way of life. The promises of salvation and eternal life come in Christ himself.

> Whoever has the Son has life; whoever does not have the

Son of God does not have life.
(1 John 5:12)

This relationship is made possible by
the presence of the *Spirit of God* in
your heart and life.

> The Spirit himself bears wit-
> ness with our spirit that we are
> children of God, and if children,
> then heirs—heirs of God and
> fellow heirs with Christ. (Rom.
> 8:16–17)

> Anyone who does not have the
> Spirit of Christ does not belong
> to him. (Rom. 8:9)

The Holy Spirit gives us power
to follow Christ (see Eph. 3:14–21),
grants us access into God's presence

through prayer (see Eph. 2:18), produces the fruit of Christian character in our lives (see Gal. 5:22–23), and enables us to understand the Scriptures (see John 14:26; 1 Cor. 2:9–13).

This new relationship with Jesus is symbolized by two practices shared by all believers: baptism and the Lord's Supper. Baptism symbolizes our union with Christ in his death, burial, and resurrection. Just as Jesus died on the cross and rose again, so also are we "buried" with Christ in baptism and raised to "walk in newness of life" (Rom. 6:4). While baptism is a one-time event that comemmorates the beginning of our Christian lives, we observe the Lord's Supper many times, when we gather with other believers to share a meal that represents Jesus's death and nourishes our faith in him (see 1 Cor. 11:23–26).

This leads to another aspect of our new life, namely our relationship with the *saints*—other followers of Jesus.

> We know that we have passed out of death into life, because we love the brothers. Whoever does not love abides in death. (1 John 3:14)

When God rescues us from sin through Jesus Christ, he makes us part of a new family—God becomes our Father, we become his children (see John 1:12–13; Gal. 3:26), and other believers in Jesus become our brothers and sisters. This family is called the church.

Membership in the church brings special privileges and responsibilities. It is our privilege to worship God, build relationships with and serve other Christians, and learn from God's Word together (see Acts 2:42–47). It is our responsibility to meet with other Christians regularly for both encouragement and help in our walk with God (see Heb. 3:12–14). This is why the writer of the letter to the Hebrews says,

> Let us hold fast the confession of our hope without wavering, for he who promised is faithful. And let us consider how to stir up one

another to love and good works,
not neglecting to meet together,
as is the habit of some, but en-
couraging one another, and all
the more as you see the Day
drawing near. (Heb. 10:23–25)

This is why every new believer should
become part of a local church, a group
of believers who are committed to following Jesus. Churches can be small
groups of people meeting in a home or
thousands of people in a huge sanctu-
ary. The size of the building and the
number of people are not what mat-
ters. What is most important is to find
a church that faithfully teaches God's
Word, practices baptism and the
Lord's Supper, and provides a context

for your spiritual growth with others
(see Eph. 4:1–16).

This, in turn, leads us to another
aspect of new life in Christ, a new relationship with the Scriptures that we
should both learn and obey.

> And by this we know that we
> have come to know him, if
> we keep his commandments.
> (1 John 2:3)

As those who have tasted the goodness
of God, we should desire the Scriptures
the way a newborn baby desires milk,
for this is how we grow (see 1 Pet.
2:1–3). God's Word is spiritual food for
the believer, the source of both nourishment and delight (see Jer. 15:16). As
we read and meditate on God's Word,

we will become spiritually healthy and strong (see Ps. 1:1–3). God's Word is the instrument God uses to make us holy (see John 17:17). As we treasure God's Word in our hearts, we will keep ourselves from sin (see Ps. 119:11). As someone once said, "Either this Book will keep you from sin, or sin will keep you from this Book."[4]

Regularly reading and studying the Scriptures is crucial for those made new in Christ. Jesus said, "If you abide in my word, you are truly my disciples, and you will know the truth, and the truth will set you free" (John 8:31–32).

Becoming the New You

As a new believer, you may wonder: *What's next? What does it mean to live the new life that comes through faith in Christ? What does he now expect from me?*

In a word: *transformation.*

God's rescue plan is not a fire insurance policy. Jesus is concerned about much more than simply delivering us from hell. He wants to restore his image within us, to make us like himself (see Rom. 8:29; Gal. 4:19). That is why Scripture puts so much emphasis on following Jesus, being his disciple, and becoming like Christ.

But becoming like Jesus is not at odds with our humanity. The truth is that we are never more ourselves than when we are like Jesus. He is, after all, the perfect picture of what it means to be fully human. As the new and better

Adam, Jesus is the clearest expression of God's image (see Col. 1:15). He radiates the glory of God, and in becoming like him, we also come to reflect his glory (see 2 Cor. 3:18).

But how does transformation happen?

It begins not in doing something new but in recognizing what God has done for you in Jesus. Your new relationship with Jesus is so close, so personal, so intimate, that God sees you *in Christ*—and Christ *in you*. This is what Jesus was teaching his disciples when he compared himself to a vine and his disciples to branches. Just as a branch derives life and nourishment from the vine and so bears fruit, so you live and produce *fruit* (meaning

God-glorifying attitudes and behavior) through your close connection to Jesus. Without him you can do nothing (see John 15:1–5).

This transformation is also what Paul was reminding his readers of when he pointed to their baptism and said that through baptism they had been buried into Jesus's death and were now raised to walk in newness of life (see Romans 6). The point is that your connection to Christ is so radical, so complete, and so profound, that your history, identity, and destiny are wrapped up in his. Your past is determined by his past: when he died on the cross for sin, it was also your death to sin's power. You have a new history. You are also identified with Jesus.

When God sees you, he sees you in the Son and treats you accordingly. Believers are sons and daughters of God precisely because they are accepted in Christ. You have a new identity. This further means that your future is secure. You will be fully transformed, so that even your physical body will be made like his (see Phil. 3:20–21). You have a new destiny. And this defines the present. Life right now is about becoming in practice more and more who we already are in Jesus.

This realization leads to new patterns of living. In one of his letters, Paul reminds believers of their new history, identity, and destiny in Jesus, and then urges them to live accordingly, setting their affections on Christ and putting sin and evil to death (see Col. 3:1–11). In other words, God wants you to be ruthless in ridding your life of sin. But this is merely the beginning. The Lord also desires you to nurture the virtues of Jesus by following his example in your attitudes and behavior, cultivating relationships in community with other believers, and allowing the gospel message to take deep root in your heart and life as you live for his name (see Col. 3:12–17).

Practically speaking, this means that the details of your life have to be reorganized around Jesus. But don't worry! The idea is not that you must now spend every waking minute in church. The point, rather, is to continually practice the presence of

God—to take notice of the Spirit's involvement in all of life, acknowledging the lordship of Jesus, and adopting his perspective and priorities as your own. Certain practices, such as praying and fasting, reading and reflecting on Scripture, serving others in your church and community, worshiping the Lord with a gathering of other believers, taking the Lord's Supper, giving to the poor, and sharing this good news with others are given precisely with this end in view. These spiritual "disciplines" are not ends in themselves but means *to* an end—the goal of being with and becoming like Jesus.

Embracing these new priorities and practices in your life will lead to increasing love for God and others. This, after all, was God's original plan: human beings who bear his image and mirror his glory by loving him with their hearts and loving others as themselves.[5]

The Story Isn't Over

The story of God's glory is an unfinished story at this point. The Lord Jesus Christ has accomplished the decisive work in God's plan to rescue the world from sin and death, but there is more to come. Followers of Jesus live in anticipation of what God has yet to do.

What is next on the horizon?

The Scriptures remind us that we are waiting for Jesus to return again.

Writing to the believers in Thessalonica, the second largest city of ancient Greece, Paul remembered "how [they] turned to God from idols to serve the living and true God, and to wait for his Son from heaven, whom he raised from the dead, Jesus who delivers us from the wrath to come" (1 Thess. 1:9–10; see also Titus 2:11–14). When Jesus comes again, our salvation will be complete (see Rom. 13:11). The New Testament constantly reminds us that we are not home yet. We are looking for the day when Jesus will physically return and make us like himself.

> But our citizenship is in heaven,
> and from it we await a Savior,
> the Lord Jesus Christ, who will

transform our lowly body to be like his glorious body, by the power that enables him even to subject all things to himself. (Phil. 3:20–21)

Beloved, we are God's children now, and what we will be has not yet appeared; but we know that when he appears we shall be like him, because we shall see him as he is. (1 John 3:2)

Like the salvation believers have already experienced in Christ, the Scriptures describe this future event in terms of new creation—God's restoration of the created world that has fallen through sin. This cosmic restoration will be nothing less than the reordering of

the entire universe under the lordship
of Jesus Christ and God his Father (see
1 Cor. 15:24–28; Eph. 1:10; Col. 1:18–
20). In the words of the prophet Isaiah,

> The wolf shall dwell with the
>   lamb,
>   and the leopard shall lie down
>   with the young goat,
> and the calf and the lion and the
>   fattened calf together;
>   and a little child shall lead
>   them. (Isa. 11:6)

The apostle John, in the final book of
the New Testament says,

> Then I saw a new heaven and a
> new earth, for the first heaven and
> the first earth had passed away,

56

and the sea was no more. And I saw the holy city, new Jerusalem, coming down out of heaven from God, prepared as a bride adorned for her husband. And I heard a loud voice from the throne saying, "Behold, the dwelling place of God is with man. He will dwell with them, and they will be his people, and God himself will be with them as their God. He will wipe away every tear from their eyes, and death shall be no more, neither shall there be mourning, nor crying, nor pain anymore, for the former things have passed away." (Rev. 21:1–4)

In the intervening time, we who follow Jesus have a mission to complete. Jesus, declaring his supreme authority over heaven and earth, left us with these instructions:

> All authority in heaven and on earth has been given to me. Go therefore and make disciples of all nations, baptizing them in the name of the Father and of the Son and of the Holy Spirit, teaching them to observe all that I have commanded you. And behold, I am with you always, to the end of the age. (Matt. 28:18–20)

This task is not yet finished. It is our great joy and privilege to finish it by going into the world in the name of the Lord Jesus Christ, sharing the good news of what he has done with others.

And this gospel of the kingdom will be proclaimed throughout the whole world as a testimony to all nations, and then the end will come. (Matt. 24:14)

And on that future day when Christ returns, "at the name of Jesus every knee should bow, in heaven and on earth and under the earth, and every tongue confess that Jesus Christ is Lord, to the glory of God the Father" (Phil. 2:10–11).

He who testifies to these things says, "Surely I am coming soon." Amen. Come, Lord Jesus! (Rev. 22:20)

Notes

1. Alisdair MacIntyre, *After Virtue: A Study in Moral Theory*, 3rd ed. (Notre Dame, IN: University of Notre Dame Press, 2007), 216.
2. Westminster Shorter Catechism, Question 1, www.opc.org/sc.html.
3. John Calvin, *Institutes of the Christian Religion*, ed. John T. McNeil, trans. Ford L. Battles, Book I, Chap. XI, 8 (Philadelphia, PA: The Westminster Press, 1960), 108.
4. This quote has been attributed to a number of Christian leaders including John Bunyan and Dwight L. Moody.
5. To learn more about the process of spiritual transformation, see my book *Christ Formed in You: The Power of the Gospel for Personal Change* (Wapwallopen, PA: Shepherd Press, 2010).

Scripture Index

Scripture Index